Other recent and forthcoming publications by Joseph Tsang Mang Kin

2008

Hakka and Huaren Destiny, Challenge and Response with a Preface by Prof Keith Lowe, PhD

A Meeting of Diasporas in Mauritius for the Indian ODI Magazine

Maurice face à son Avenir : Une vision et une Grande Ambition, in Mauritius Times

Beginnings of our Foreign Affairs - An Insider's view in Mauritius - 40 Years After – New Goals, New Challenges, published by the Government of Mauritius.

To be published in January 2009
(by the President's Fund for Creative Writing in English)

Stopovers in a Poet's Mind - 150 sonnets

And the following to be published in February & March 2009
by Editions de l'Ocean Indien:

Political and Social Chronologies of Mauritius from 1507 to 1992.

Three Essays on Sir Seewoosagur Ramgoolam, Father of the Nation

Destins croisés auprès de Raymond Chasle, Professeur, Poète et Diplomate

Entering the Chinese Mind
and other Sonnets

Joseph Tsang Mang Kin

CPTM
LONDON

First published in Great Britain in 2008 CPTM

Copyright © Joseph Tsang Mang Kin 2008

The moral right of the author has been asserted.

All rights reserved.

No part of this publication may be reproduced,
stored in a retrieval system, or transmitted, in any form or by
any means, without prior permission in writing of the publisher, nor be
otherwise circulated in any form of binding or cover other than that in which it
is published and without a similar condition including this condition being
imposed on the subsequent purchaser.

A CIP Catalogue record for this book
is available from the British Library.

ISBN-13: 978-0-9554402-1-2

CPTM Ltd
63 Catherine Place
London, SWE1 6DY
www.cptm.org

smart.partnership@cptm.org

Cover Picture: "Entering the Chinese Mind" by Michel Darmon

Joe's sonnets, dedicated to Smart Partners, demonstrate the function of Art, Science and Philosophy in serving one's wish to round off, or complete the gripping uncertainty of the complex global dynamic and of the interface between Smart Partners experiences and ideas with which one seeks out new experiences, cultures and change.

Dr Mihaela Y. Smith. PJN, KMN
Joint Dialogue Convener & CEO
CPTM Smart Partners' Hub, London

The Smart Partnership Movement anchored by CPTM has been linking people and ideas through distinct ongoing dialogues in an "open house" approach combining science with co-operative governance, economics and culture since 1984. The Smart Partnership dialogues are enriched through the synchronisation of values and issues, articulated through tradition and modernity, art and culture, initiated in 2001 in Munyonyo, Uganda and carried forward through the African, Caribbean, West Asian and Mediterranean Webs to Mulungushi, Zambia in 2008. In 2005, CPTM has also published "Let the cat turn round: one man's traverse of the Twentieth Century" by Dr Alexander King, CPTM Co-Founder and member of the Club of Rome.

'In Joseph Tsang Mang Kin's anthology of sonnets, readers are provided with an interpretation of an Old World culture which bears extreme relevance to this day due to its unique value as a moral document rather than a mere historical review of myths and legends of earliest antiquity. The poet's creative process evolves from his firm grasp of his own racial identity and consciousness. For instance, he shows his appreciation for many aspects of his parent culture, e.g. his benevolent forebears, the Chinese belief system, their concept of harmony as two equal parts of a whole (Yin and Yang), and most importantly the need to recognise the group as against the individual in assessing human rights. In a rich harvest of recollections, coloured by many fluid images in his lyrical verse, and certainly not compromised by someone else's translation, the poet takes great pride in the tools of language he inherited to facilitate his emergence as a bilingual poet and essayist. The work ends on a note of pride and industry, and may be considered timeless. It demonstrates in a convincing manner that a proper understanding of the cultural values existing in Mauritius today must be based upon an appreciation of the history of the movement of people into that country from other parts of the world.'

- Mrs Kean Springer, Musician & Author, Barbados

Joseph Tsang Mang Kin is a very imaginative poet. In this book, when one reads any of his sonnets, one craves to read the next and then the next, and so forth till all are read. Each sonnet leaves the reader with a wonderful pictorial image lingering in the mind. Such is the power of the author's highly informative messaging.

- Professor Heneri A M Dzinotyiweyi, Director of Gutsameso Art Gallery & MP, Zimbabwe

These beautifully crafted poems give us an intriguing insight into the differences in perception between the religious basis of Abrahamic societies and the secular humanism which underpins Chinese culture. These sonnets also explore the sensibilities of the Chinese diaspora in countries such as Mauritius where people from all the regions of the world met and melded into new nations and nationalities and absorbed new concepts which will resonate with many because they have become such an integral part of our globalized lives.

- Mrs Patsy Robertson, Jamaica

Foreword

Mauritius is indeed a privileged meeting place of all the main cultures of the world which all come from the Northern Hemisphere, with the exception of Africa. Our public holidays include four main festivals namely the Chinese New Year, the Indian Divali, the Christian Christmas and the Muslim End of Ramadan, which are celebrated throughout the island.

Accustomed from our childhood to witness or participate in the celebrations of different religious ceremonies concerning births, weddings or funerals, and to absorb and respect them, the Mauritian is a born citizen of the world. He has learnt not from books, but from real life situations what it means to be a Buddhist, a Christian Hindu or a Muslim. Without being a specialist of any of these religions, he knows the dos and don'ts, and most important, the cultural and invisible bounds he should not cross. He knows the differences and the similarities which a monocultural or monolingual foreigner does not see or understand. And this is where Mauritians are immediately aware of mistakes committed by world leaders trying to deal with peoples of different backgrounds and culture, living in different parts of the world.

Mauritius is a place where you can compare religions and cultures. While the European sees the Asian with a European eyes and mind values and prejudices; the Asian sees the European with Asian eyes, his own values and prejudices. But this, more importantly, can be a vantage point where the Mauritian can see the European world and ideas with a Mauritian /Asian mind and can also see the Asian world and ideas, with a Mauritian/Asian mind.

This is where I came to see the difference between the Chinese and the European understanding of each other, and sought to identify the causes of this misunderstanding. They do not know each other. They do not have the same background and education. They do not know each other's culture. They do not have the same Genesis, the same beginnings; the Western man has inherited a Middle Eastern culture, from Akkadia, and a prophet by the name of Abraham. The Chinese have no such religious beginnings.

Theirs is a secular humanism and culture that comes from the banks of Yang Tze and Huang He and is completely different from the Akkadian culture born in the desert near Euphrates and Tigris which produced the three revealed religions: Judaism, Christianity and Islam. Chinese history has no account of encounters with deities, served by angels or sending out messengers to convey their orders to mankind. But the Chinese have their own myths of origin, their Genesis, Fuxi and Nuwa, their own understanding or reading of the purpose of existence and their duties towards life, themselves and their environment.

This anthology` can be divided into three unequal parts: the first one groups sonnets that each capture a specific aspect of Chinese culture, myth, philosophy, festivals and human rights; the second groups three sonnets that try to explain the origins of two minority languages namely Cantonese and Hakka which were downgraded to help the promotion and supremacy of mandarin or Putonghua, and the last part explains the role of the Chinese in Mauritius. Where they settled in Port-Louis soon became known as Chinatown, with a Chinese Chamber of Commerce, pagodas, clan clubs, Chinese restaurants, shops and pharmacies. This is the place that gave birth to the very first industries in Mauritius.

Joseph Tsang Mang Kin
Mauritius
June 2008

Contents

Entering The Chinese Mind	2
Yin and Yang	4
Genesis	6
Sacred Scriptures	8
Fuxi and Nuwa - First Parents	10
The First Lesson	12
Shang Di	14
The Yellow Emperor	16
Self Sacrifice	18
Confucius and Lao Zi	20
Honour To Confucius	22
Honour To Lao Zi	24
Not To Be Named	26
Man Or Butterfly	28
Meditation	30
River Dragon	32
Why Number Eight	34
Guan Di	36
Toleration	38
Why Zheng He Stopped Sailing	40
Fu Lu Shou	42
Chinese New Year	44
Seven Teas	46
Lantern Festival	48
Without Voting	50
Our Human Rights	52
Ai Guo Or Love Of Nation	54
Clash Of Culture	56
Hakka Language	58
Cantonese and Hakka	60
Cantonese, Hakkanese and Mandarin	62
Chinatown 1938	64
Xin-Fa In The Forties	66
The Powerhouse	68
Chinatown Today	70

1.

ENTERING THE CHINESE MIND

As you enter, leave Sacred Books outside:
We have no God that's warlike or jealous
We have no hell where the sinful will burn
And no virgins waiting for us up there.

We can't confirm God is One or Many
Helped by angels or sending messengers.
We don't even say that we have a soul
To save from sins we committed, unborn.

Who can for sure tell us the difference
Between sane creeds and wild superstitions?
That's why we don't convert nor colonize:
We have no jihads, no Inquisition.

What we dream of we create here and now.
We pursue Happiness, Wealth and Long Life.

2.

YIN AND YANG

It was the "With Name", the Great Name-able
All that can be known and the mind can grasp,
A waving line passing through a Circle
Such as we represent the "Without Name"
The Great Unname-able, all that exists
With no beginning, no end, stretching
Beyond infinity, dimensionless,
That brought about the two halves that we name
Yang, the light, positive and masculine
Yin, the dark, negative and feminine,
Each pole breeding a dot that grows into
It's opposite, all being One and Change.

At our gates, Yang Lion under its paw
Holds the Globe, while Yin Lion keeps a cub.

3.

GENESIS

In the beginning, **TAO**, One, the Mover
Engendered the infinite empty space:
No Heaven, no Earth, no Shape. Images
Of endless depths, darkness, desolation…
Then Two dashed out, soon to be Yin and Yang
Both plaiting Heaven's web and Earth's lifelines.

Out of the boundless egg **PANGU** was born
A spirit in Heaven and a saint on Earth.
His breath became the wind; his voice, thunder;
His left eye, the sun; his right eye, the moon;
His bones, stones; his marrow, pearls and jade;
His whiskers, stars; his blood, the Huang He;
Sweat, rain and body hair, vegetation.

In Chinese lore, that's how it all began.

4.

SACRED SCRIPTURES

Children of the Dragon! O Han People!
Blessed you are that your sacred Scriptures
Told you no tales of thunder-mouthed deities
Hounding their brood, threatening damnation
Demanding bloodshed to appease their ire.

Lucky you are indeed that from the start
You had no odd visionary that claimed
Privileged contacts with eerie Powers
That dictate orders and exact compliance.

Lucky indeed that your Holy Scriptures
Started with the One that brought Yin and Yang.
So from the dawn of life the first teaching
Is how to flow and be one with the Chi [i]
To merge opposites and be Ta-Yi [ii].

5.

FUXI AND NUWA - FIRST PARENTS

Blessed we are that Fuxi and Nuwa
Our first parents were not kicked out of home,
Had no knowledge of sin, shame or blackmail.
So the Couple formed sane parents and guides.

Fuxi holding the square of rectitude
Taught their children animal husbandry
Gave them the fishing net and the ba-gua [iii]
That helps access collective unconscious.

Nuwa with compasses of good measure
Instituted marriage and played the lute.
Next came agriculture with picks and ploughs
And we were taught how plants and herbs can heal.

Useful tools and teachings that's what we got.
Bullyings or killings never were our lot.

6.

THE FIRST LESSON

Readers of tortoise shells, O Han people!
How wonderful that from the beginning
The One opened it up as Yin and Yang
And gave you eight trigrams to access it.

The first Couple, our parents, were sane guys
Father Fuxi demanding, principled,
Mother Nu Wa caring, soft and loving
Female and male, equals, like Yin and Yang

Fortunate indeed that your earliest books
Taught self respect, empathy with Nature
Healthy food and sex life to ripe old age
And the secrets of the Way and Virtue.

We never learnt to feel hatred for life
But to love it and make the most of it.

7.

SHANG DI

Shang Di's the name we give to the Unknown,
The Utmost Spirit, the topmost Deity
Who has an earthly image in our midst
The Emperor or the Son of Heaven.

Heaven, Mankind and Earth represented
By three horizontal lines when connected
By a vertical pole, a hieroglyph
Read as Wang, the backbone of Existence.

The monarch has a mandate to protect
All his subjects from hunger and dangers
And ensure compliance with divine will
So harmony under heaven stays whole.

But when chaos lets loose famine or wars
It means he's failed and must vacate the throne.

8.

THE YELLOW EMPEROR

My Soukpo [iv] told me so much about him [v]
I thought he was an Uncle in China
Waiting for us to go there and thank him
For the wonderful things he did for us.

He took the uncouth tribes on Huang-He banks
From the dark Stone Age to civilisation.
His inventions do show how much he cared:
Writing, arithmetic, the calendar,

Land parcelling for cultivation,
Raising of silkworm to produce silk,
Clothing, music, building of palaces,
Making of carts and boats plus the compass.

That's how we came to think of our leaders
Not as warriors but sages and teachers.

9.

SELF SACRIFICE

Self sacrifice is as old as Huang He.
Who has not heard of Yu the flood fighter?
He left his wife three days after wedding
But toiled year in year out constructing dams.
Now when he was before his home, would not
Stop work, go in and hug his newborn son.

Every one knows the Great Wall that was built
To keep away wild hordes of invaders.
So to protect collective interest
Each family had to donate a son
To pile up the boulders knowing full well
He'll die of exhaustion within the year.

You lay down your life not to save your soul
But that others may continue to live.

10.

CONFUCIUS AND LAO ZI

Confucius and Lao Zi are the two sides
Of the same Chinese personality
The two teachers who modelled the Han mind
Cannot like the Yin and Yang be disjoined.

The first taught rules for social intercourse:
Always respect others and keep your word
Not for rewards nor punishments, simply
To enjoy the trip without accidents.

Lao Zi looking beyond everyday life
Found silence, non action, the inner path
That leads to the core of being – the One
A unique one each one must tread alone.

Our Sages signposted the Goal to reach
In the limelight and with the inner light.

11.

HONOUR TO CONFUCIUS

You seem so far away and yet you stand
Midway between today and our Forebears
Whose wisdom of five millennia ago
You salvaged, and handed down to us.

You laid down the rules of good behaviour
Centred on the family then spreading
Out to the clan, society and the world
To build up brotherhood on truth and trust.

How wonderful that your teachings were not
Based on blackmail, fierce threats or punishments!
But on honour, logic, mutual respect
So we make life easy and smooth for all:

In a nutshell: Don't do unto others
What you don't wish others to do to you.

12.

HONOUR TO LAO ZI

That guy that disappeared behind the pass
Has grasped the Way and the Virtues of Tao
He who speaks does not know so then indeed
Because you do not speak I know you knew.

But not much for sure since no mortal mind can
Contain eternity that cannot be
Contained within time-space continuum
As it sits inside and outside all bounds.

But still I know you know much more as I
Watch you seated tranquil with red mei flowers
In hand on your black mule trotting up and
Down the slippery frost of my wall paper.

The world will swirl and twirl and whirl
But one with the One, each one is the All.

13.

NOT TO BE NAMED

Not to be named indeed you would prefer!
Having chosen to shed your outer self,
Outside limelight, aspiring to be sucked
Out of existence and merged with the One.

For sure amidst the leaves and butterflies
That mope in and out between here and there
On the morning mountain tops of my mind
I know you're there Lao Zi, Old child, Wise Guy.

You sit mute on your mule near the threshold
To the Other side but not yet stepping
Into the Absolute, the No name, Tao.
Quiet, peaceful and reconciled with Life.

The path we need follow is inside us.
But rushing elsewhere will take us nowhere.

14.

MAN OR BUTERFLY

I, Zhuang Zi [vi] dreamt I was a butterfly
Flitting around or seeming unconscious
Bathing unsubstantial in deep delight.
I was simply a happy butterfly
Flying with no knowledge that I could be
Or not anything save a butterfly.

Then all of a sudden I came off sleep
And discovered I was Zhuang Zi again,
The guy I was before I fell asleep.
Am I dreaming I am a butterfly
Or am I now for sure a butterfly
Dreaming it is Zhuang Zi, no one can tell.

Are we real? Or just an illusion?
An endless flow of metamorphoses?

15.

MEDITATION

On the rose-perfumed breath of dream light
Poised like the lotus closed, inside ablaze
In the inner centre of your deep self
Where time slows down to a stop and a dot.

Dance and merge with the butterflies
Flowing in and out of the bamboo stirs.
You seem to see silence breathe till no sound
Is heard and disappears, a fleeting sheet.

No Light. Nor darkness either, and no Self.
But an expanse timeless where galaxies
Are motionless as if time stopped but still
Moving around itself untrapped, mindless.

No coming! No going. Just there. Nowhere.
Depth and the Void, ecstatic and static.

16.

RIVER DRAGON

River Dragon you grew out of our dreams
From the dark deepest roots and shoots of time
Pouring on our forebears life-giving rains
As now you do sky-scraping, nose-diving.

You have the mane and tail of a lithe steed
Horns of a deer, paws of dogs, scales of fish
And your body is a long lissom snake,
O unbound totem, our magic emblem!

Dragon invisible, so near so dear,
None will believe nor ever know you're here
With us, inside and outside our minds
A live vortex of frenzied firecrackers.

None will divine you're our roller-coaster
As we sit and ride on your restless tail.

17.

WHY NUMBER EIGHT

Why we love number eight? Simply because
It's the meeting-place of Chinese wisdom:
First we have the Ba Gua, the Eight Trigrams
That open the gates to the Supreme Mind.

Next Confucius taught Eight Rules of Conduct:
Filial piety, politeness, decorum,
Integrity, faithfulness, modesty
Brotherly attention and loyalty.

Then Buddha had on the sole of his feet
The Eight auspicious signs: the Wheel of Law,
The Conch Shell, the Umbrella, Canopy
Lotus, Jar, Fishes and the Mystic Knot.

Last but not least [vii] eight Taoist free-thinkers
Became Ba Xian [viii] or the Eight Immortals.

18.

GUAN DI

Like all settlers carrying their deities
The Chinese who arrived in a foreign country
Would have a shrine in their shops, then would build
A Temple dedicated to Guan Di .

A General that helped Han Emperor,
Liu Pei, clear the country of thieves and thugs.
After his death he was made Immortal
And to this day is remembered and loved.

He taught us to practise the Eight virtues:
Loyalty, righteousness, sincerity,
Courage, grandeur, uprightness, honesty
And honour to make like pleasurable.

Guan Di is a symbol and Patron Saint
Who inspires and binds our Diaspora

19.

TOLERATION

They say you have to believe in something
Or some god, I'm not sure! That's the mindset
From Mesopotamia, but look around
At some other cultures, say, the Chinese.

We go to the Temple to offer food
And mock money to our dear ones next door.
For sure, we ask them to look after us
Bring us good health also material wealth.

There's no way to explain how they can help
As no one holds the key to afterlife.
All that's certain is our uncertainties
Thenceforth no need for creeds that hatred breed.

Beliefs commit none else but believers.
Why not put up with each other's errors?

20.

WHY ZHENG HE STOPPED SAILING

We might for ever be wondering why
After circumnavigating the world
Some eighty years ahead of Da Gama
Or any sailor from Christian Europe,
The Ming Dynasty inexplicably
Terminated Zheng He's [ix] expeditions.

But there's a clue if we ask why the West
- Portugal, Spain, Holland, France and Britain -
Let loose their conquerors across wild waves.
So many things they lacked like land and gold
But had divine sanction [x] to raid and grab
Plus a mission to convert the Pagans [xi].

The Ming had no Gospel to teach the world
And deemed the world had nothing to offer.

21.

FU LU SHOU[xii]

I celebrate Fu Lu Shou, our Three Stars
The ultimate Blessings for life on earth:

Fu, happiness merges body and soul.
So the ideogram shows on the left
An Altar with offerings to Heaven
And on the right one mouth close to paddies.

Lu is the summit of accomplishment
Resulting from scholarly pursuits
And rewarded as in imperial days
With fame, honours and a hefty pension.

And **Shou**, long life to enjoy Fu and Lu[xiii]
So we can hold the cup of wine always
To celebrate till ripe old age then leave[xiv]
Content while our loved ones can feast in peace[xv].

22.

CHINESE NEW YEAR

All debts are cleared before the New Year starts.
We assemble at the Temple amidst
Our Ancestors and Gods for Thanksgiving
And present them with pork, fish and chicken.

Then to Chao Shen on his way to Heaven,
We offer loads of sweets, cake and honey
So he makes nice reports on us and brings
Back happiness, good fortune and long life.

For our safety we have many Gate Gods [xvi]
Stern Vi Tse Kung and smiling Chung Shiuk
There to wipe out both ill luck and illness,
While the whole clan enjoys its ten-course feast.

Rich with foungpaos [xvii] children can play "Van lak" [xviii]
And get a first taste of the whims of fate.

23.

SEVEN TEAS[xix]

The popular puli a black tea, rich dark brown
In colour from Yunnan helps digestion.

Green teas like Oolong or Tikuanyin are
Dried up in silver basins placed on fire.

Yellow teas are those silvery needles
from Junsan or yellow shoots from Fuksan.

The smooth lungching, or clear dragon-well tea
Produced for royalty comes from Hanchow.

Shou mei the white tea nurtured in Fujian
Has the sweet taste of white peony flowers.

When you mix Jasmine and Chrysanthemun
Flowers with green tea you get moliche.

And from Guangdong hongche or the red tea
Alone can be drunk with milk and sugar.

24.

LANTERN FESTIVAL

Then after a fortnight merry making,
Visiting relatives, welcoming friends
We have some more feasting also gambling
And congregate to close celebrations.

All the neighbours join in a procession
Of animals carried with bamboo sticks:
Fishes with flowing tails softly rippling
And tortoises of long and healthy life,

Each one shining from a candle inside
Draped in muslin paper of all colours
But the restless dragon twelve metres long
Keeps on their toes a crowd of kungfu boys.

In an endless thunder of firecrackers
We roam the streets till Pagoda's in sight.

25.

WITHOUT VOTING

For millennia we've lived without voting
Without choosing our Chiefs or Emperors.
Entrusted with a Mandate from Heaven
They have to feed and protect their people.

For centuries they have done their duties
To the people who always trusted them
But when they failed, as it happened sometimes
The naked and hungry pushed them away.

We've never known or cared about voting
Once in a while every four or five years.
What we demand is our bowls of rice,
Clothes for us all and a roof on our heads.

Leaders and led know each other's station
And work as one man to build the Nation.

26.

OUR HUMAN RIGHTS

Democracy for us means human rights
Not for individuals but for the group
That should always come first and be prepared
To sacrifice persons for its own survival.

Individuals have no personal claims
Outside the clans that give him existence,
As trees we need water and oxygen
Not for one tree but for the whole forest.

We've lived in groups from times immemorial
And survived floods and invasions.
So when Mao imposed the straightjacket
The world could see an ocean of blue ants.

The clan comes first, brothers next, ego last.
That's how we write the three parts of our names.

27.

AI GUO OR LOVE OF NATION

We need not know where our leaders come from.
They have been there long before we arrived
And they will continue like the mountains
To stay after we're gone, they're part of life.

Royals and commoners that never mix
Band together whenever in danger
To stop hordes of invaders from Outside
Or the Rivers flooding plains and paddies.

The psyche that two millennia ago
Caused the Great Wall to grow and stop Xiongnus
Now stirs and drives both guides and followers
To show the world it's now their turn to shine.

Whatever our feelings for the leaders
In them we trust, in trust we grow with them.

28.

CLASH OF CULTURE

We never thought highly of your culture
That never helped you out of poverty,
Nor were you proud of what you were before
Owned by feudal lamas we neutralized.
No longer serfs but citizens set free.
No need for you to crawl in dirt or dust
And beg for food and a decent living.

Now you have new houses and railways
To connect you to civilisation.
Why do you need to cling to useless creeds?
Why can't you understand we close temples
To assist you combat superstition ?
How can you be so ungrateful and not
Appreciate we want you to be like us?

29.

HAKKA LANGUAGE

Make no mistake: our Hakka language
Predates all the Mandarin dialects.
It was spoken in the Kingdom of Qi [xx]
The very last to be destroyed by Qin [xxi].

Seeking safety some Qi-nese fled Eastward
To Kow Li [xxii] that preserved down to this day
Familiar words like kyo-yuk [xxiii] at tae-hak [xxiv]
Or to Japan where they wrapped up [xxv] our sounds.

Those who fled South changed their names, hid their ranks
But their language survived and resurfaced
With the Tang dynasty whose palaces
For centuries echoed our ancient tongue.

We knew we kept intact the true language.
Today they say we've kept the culture too [xxvi].

30.

CANTONESE AND HAKKA

Cantonese is the Chinese coelacanth
Nurtured by the millions of deportees
From the Great Wall to the Deep south Coastline [xxvii]
Amidst jagged crags and rough rivers where
They maintained most ancient sounds and tones
Resisting invasion from Southern barbarians.

Hakka people escaping genocide
Fled East and South, and commuting between
The two rivers [xxviii] over a millennium
Found their haven in the Tang Palaces
Where the five-word quatrain [xxix] with three endings
That rhyme in our Hakka down to this day.

Both Cantonese and Hakka folk believe
They are the only Tang that have survived.

31.

CANTONESE, HAKKANESE AND MANDARIN

Now safe and sound in the southern surround
The Nam Shun preserved the precious speech:
All nineteen initials, seven vowels,
Six finals and the distinctive eight tones.

But the flat North soon overrun by hordes
Found ancient tones scaled down to six
While Hakkanese in Central plains lost two
More initials, one vowel and two tones.

But both have kept the same ancient endings[xxx]:
-p, -t, -k -m, that make Tang poetry rhyme
Ceased to exist in Mandarin dialects
When they interacted with alien tongues.

Cantonese and hakka are true "Tong Fa[xxxi]"
Unmauled, unmaimed quite unlike mandarin

32.

CHINATOWN 1938

Born on the Twelfth of March in Chinatown...
Born at midday in a Temple compound...

'Twas thirty years before Independence:
No TV, no radio, no computers,
No cars but carts, man-pulled or donkey-drawn
With osier-caged roosters, merry-choiring.

Families went to Koong Chin [xxxii] for film shows
And weddings sealed with three face-to-face bows
Or Pagodas amidst smoking joss sticks
To greet Ancestors or chat with our Gods.

Toddlers stuck to their mums but teenagers
Preferred Chan Chak [xxxiii] where basketball was sweet
Excuse for tickled hearts to exchange smiles,
None of us knew we lived in Paradise.

33.

XIN-FA IN THE FORTIES

Life centred on Xinfa: each day began
With the anthem and salute to the flag
And kids proudly holding their wooden guns
In their military fatigues and caps.

While we carved soap into miniature tanks
With no idea what real ones could do
We loved to hear that one-string violin
Pleading at night for Moy-Kong[xxxiv] to flow there.

But soon the war thousands of miles away
Was breaking up our school and families
Ruining all hopes of old age in Moy-Yen.

Whichever side they backed, the supporters
Were stuck on their island, stateless, until
Independence made them all Mauritians.

34.

THE POWERHOUSE

This is the place that gave birth to it all.
Prompted by threatening German warships
That kept away our needed rice and wares,
The Chinese here produced the foods and goods.

At home we made our noodles and tofu
Brewed demijohns of fish and soya sauce
Salted hamchoy down, churned out sausages
And turned tired tyres into flipflops

With wars, our homes grew into factories
That produced lemonade, wine and biscuits,
Soap, wax, matches, cigarettes, furniture
Canvas and leather shoes and umbrellas.

That powerhouse that launched our industries
Chinatown, covers less than a square mile.

35.

CHINATOWN TODAY

Now forty years after Independence:
The narrow streets suffocate with traffic.
Walls are pulled down for access to car parks
While vegetable stalls hide the pavements.

The CCC[xxxv] went up in smoke with all
Our Immigrants' histories and memories
But Heen Foh[xxxvi], Xin Fa[xxxvii] and the Book Club
Keep lively company with restaurants.

All spread language, culture and traditions
Like Alumnis active at Chung San Hall[xxxviii]
Or new Heritage Court that pays tribute
To great Nam Soon leader, Affan Tank Wen[xxxix].

Here our minds and our hearts will, for ever,
Between two triumphal arches, live on.

End Notes

i) Chi in Chinese means the breath or Prana in sanscrit of the deity or God

ii) Ta-Yi is the Great One or the Great Unity, the Absolute. It is not an entity and has nothing to do with an anthropological concept

iii) Pa Kua are the Eight Hexagrams that form the I Ching

iv) Sookpo . In Hakka, the Grand Aunt on the Mother's side.

v) According to tradition, he is supposed to have acceded the throne in 2697 BC

vi) According to the Historical Records of Sima Qian (c.145-c.89 BC), Zhuang Zi lived in the reigns of King Hui of Liang or Wei (370-319 BC) and King Xuan of Ch'I (319-301BC). Joseph Needham in Science and Civilisation in China gives his dates as 369-286BC. He is supposed to have come from the district of Meng in the present province of Henan, and held a private post in the Lacquer Garden, which he abandoned for private life. He is fond of mocking logic, scorning office and wealth and ecstatically contemplating death as part of the universal process of Nature (A C Graham).

vii) **Guan Di** or **Kwan Ti** (160- 220 AD) a warrior became a legendary figure after his death and was promoted to a heavenly position as Lord of Literature. He taught the Eight Principles taught by Guan Di which are: Loyalty, Sincerity, Righteousness, Courage, Uprightness, Grandeur, Honour and Honesty. There are also the Eight magnificent horses or the eight kinds of musical sounds as reproduced from: the calabash, earthenware, stretched hides, wool, stone, metal, silk strings and bamboo.

viii) Xian were men who had been united to the Tao. They are now Immortals and live in the world of Eternal Bliss and can wander on Earth and in Heaven. Among them, the most famous are: **Ba Xian**, (or Eight Immortals) namely Li Teguai, Nan Zhongli, Zhang Guolo, He Xiangu, Lan Caihe, Lu Dongbin and Cao Guoju. Each one carries a treasure, eight in all.

ix) **Zheng He** originally named Ma Sanbao (马三保), was born in 1371 of the Hui ethnic group and the Muslim faith in modern-day Yunnan Province, one of the last possessions of the Mongols of the Yuan Dynasty before being conquered by the Ming Dynasty. He served as a close confidant of the Yongle Emperor of China (reigned 1403–1424), the third emperor of the Ming Dynasty. Zheng He's ancestors include a general for Genghis Khan. Between 1405 and 1433, the Ming government sponsored a series of seven naval expeditions. Emperor **Yongle** designed them to establish a Chinese presence, impose imperial control over trade, and impress foreign peoples in the Indian Ocean basin. Zheng He was placed as the admiral in control of the huge fleet and armed forces that undertook these expeditions. Subsequently, for no known reason the Imperial officials gave up any plans to maintain a Chinese presence in the Indian Ocean and even destroyed most of the nautical charts that Zheng He had carefully prepared. The decommissioned treasure ships sat in harbours until they rotted away, and Chinese craftsmen forgot the technology of building such large vessels.

x) On 4 May 1493 **Pope Alexander VI Borgia** issued the Inter Coetera Bull amending the Aeterna Regis Bull of 1481 of Sixtus IV granting to the Portuguese alone the right to conquer the world. Inter caetera states: "… we (the Papacy) command you (Spain) … to instruct the aforesaid inhabitants and residents and dwellers therein in the Catholic faith, and train them in good morals." This papal command marked the beginning of colonisation and Catholic missions the New World and elsewhere. Now the Pope had divided the new world between the Spanish and the Portuguese by drawing a line from pole to pole (hence, Brazil speaks Portuguese today, and the rest of Latin Americas speaks Spanish). The Dutch, the French and the British were not in the picture.

The slave trade that developed was so profitable that the others joined in, like Sir Francis Drake.

xi) Zheng He became known in the West after the publication of **Gavin Menzies** book: 1421, in which he says that Zheng He in that year, long before **Vasco Da Gama**, sailed round the world. He went on seven expeditions in the Indian Ocean with each fleet consisting of between 50 to100 junks and 20,000 Men. His vessels were 300 feet long whereas **Colombus**'s Santa Maria was only 90 feet long. Zheng He is said to have served as the model for Sindbad the Sailor.

xii) In most Chinese homes, one can find the three statues of this holy trinity, known as the Three Stars (San Xing). They are not deities but embodiments of the ultimate blessings that a Chinese would aspire to, and which will make his life meaningful: Happiness, Success and Longevity. The Hakka and Cantonese read : Fuk, Luk Shou.

If he is lucky or fortunate enough he will live till very old age, in good health and prosperity.

xiii) It is interesting to note that the Fu and Lu have homophones meaning, a bat and a stag. That's why the Chinese are fond of these animals in carvings.

So when he passes away, he does not expect his family to pass their time in mourning, although he will not be able to prevent his loved ones from regretting his absence.

xv) That is why after the funeral of an elder who lived a happy or well fulfilled life, the family and clan gather the same evening for a banquet in his honour. Death being part of Life, a new page is turned. Life continues.

xvi) Gate gods or mun shîn are numerous. The most popular among Hakkas are Yü Th'ih Kung and Ch'in Yüan Shuai. Refer to: Chinese Gods – Unseen World of Spirits and Demons, Collins & Brown, HK 1997.

xvii)   Red envelopes containing money.
xix)   Play cards, gamble.
xx)   Inspired by Professor Shiu L Kong's Book: Chinese Culture and Lore.
xxi)   Qi in putonghua and in other transliteration systems is written Ch'I.
xxii)   Qin was the First Emperor.
xxiii) Kow Li is Korea.
xxiv)   Kyo yuk: manners or education
xxiv)   Say moy and thai hok, meaning miss or young lady in Hakka have the same sounds and meanings in the Korean language. In mandarin, these words become xiao jie or da xue.

xxv) Japanese has two sets of numbers from one to ten one of Japanese and the other of Chinese Hakka derivation. For example: one or yit in hakka becomes ichi; two in hakka is ni, same sound in Japanese but in mandarin; four in hakka in see, in Japanese it's shi, but sz in mandarin nine in Hakka is kiu, same in Japanese, whereas in mandarin it is jiu.

xxvi) According to **Xie Xiaodong**, associate professor from School of Life Sciences, Lanzhou University, pure Hans don't exist anymore, but the ancient culture has been kept by the Hakka people.

xxvii) The T'sie Yun dictionary published in 601AD records the language spoken in the old capital Chang An in 600 AD. At about the same time **Lu DeMing** who died in 630AD published his King tien shi wen dictionary. Based on these works, which added to his own findings in1940 and subsequent research, which culminated in Grammatica Sinica Recensa, published Sweden 1957, reprinted Udevala 1987, **sinologist Bernard Karlgren**, (1889-1978) has come up with a fine key to the different pronuncations and tones of Chinese ideograms in Archaic Chinese, Middle Chinese and mandarin today.

We have confirmation that what in the North, eventually became the Mandarin languages had ancient form endings in –p, -t, -m and –k.

xxviii) Huang He and Yangzikiang.

xxix) A favourite format with Tang poets like Li Pai or Tu Fu

xxx) For example , if we take the numbers one to ten read in Hakka, with endings in –p, -t, -m and –k, we find that in Ancient Chinese number ten (soup) ends with a –p sound, number one(yit) and eight (pat)t, end with a –t sound, three (sam) with a –m sound, and six (liuk)ends with a -k sound. All these endings disappeared in modern mandarin now known as putonghua, the national language. So there is no doubt that Cantonese and Hakkaares related to an older form of Chinese than the Mandarin dialects including putonghua.

xxxi) Tong Fa in Hakkanese means Tang Tongue, the language of the Tang dynasty.

xxxii) A hall for social gatherings, in Chinatown.

xxxiii)The seat of the Chan Clan with a temple and a playground. It served as a very popular meeting place for celebrations and sports in the Sixties.

xxxiv) Moy Kong is the River Moy in hakka land, that is Moy-yen or Meixian in mandarin, formerly known as Kai-ying chou, the seat of hakka learning in the Guangdong Province.

xxxv) CCC: Chinese Chamber of Commerce. All the documents pertaining to the arrival of the Chinese immigrants went in smoke in the fire in 1996.

xxxvi) Heen Foh, a Chinese Association that from the 1940 chose to side with Communist Mao against Nationalist Chiang.

xxxvii) Xin Fa: New China, the name of the School run by Heen Foh.

xxxviii)Chinese Cultural Centre, founded by former Minister Jean Ah Chuen, known to be pro Taiwan.

xxxix) He was the second leader of the Chinese community. He arrived in Mauritius, married a Sino-creole Christian, Elizabeth Athow, was noticed by Governor John Pope Hennessy who appointed in the Constitutional Reform Committee. Businessman and philanthropist, he was much respected by the whole Mauritian Community.